No Lex 11-12

Patrick Henry

SPIRIT
of America®

PATRICK *Henry*

ORATOR AND PATRIOT

By Ann Heinrichs

Content Advisers: John and Amy Kukla, Red Hill, The Patrick Henry
National Memorial, Brookneal, Virginia

The Child's World®
Chanhassen, Minnesota

6

PATRICK *Henry*

Published in the United States of America by The Child's World®
P.O. Box 326 • Chanhassen, MN 55317-0326 • 800-599-READ • www.childsworld.com

Acknowledgments
The Child's World®: Mary Berendes, Publishing Director

Editorial Directions, Inc.: E. Russell Primm, Editorial Director; Pam Rosenberg, Line Editor; Katie Marsico, Assistant Editor; Matthew Messbarger, Editorial Assistant; Susan Hindman, Copy Editor; Susan Ashley, Proofreader; Julie Zaveloff, Chris Simms, and Peter Garnham, Fact Checkers; Tim Griffin/IndexServ, Indexer; Dawn Friedman, Photo Researcher; Linda S. Koutris, Photo Selector

The Design Lab: Kathleen Petelinsek, Art Direction; Kari Thornborough, Page Production

Photo
Cover: North Wind Picture Archives; National Portrait Gallery, Smithsonian Institution/Art Resource, NY: 8, 28; Bettmann/Corbis: 10, 18; Corbis: 17; Lee Snider/Corbis: 24; Archivo Iconografico, S.A./Corbis: 25; The Granger Collection, New York: 6, 11, 12, 13, 23; Hulton\Archive/Getty Images: 27; North Wind Picture Archives: 2, 7, 15, 16, 20, 21; Stock Montage, Inc.: 22.

Library of Congress Cataloging-in-Publication Data
Heinrichs, Ann.
  Patrick Henry : orator and patriot / by Ann Heinrichs.
    p. cm. — (Our people)
Includes bibliographical references and index.
Contents: Seven awesome words—Treason, liberty, and death—Fighting for rights—United we stand.
  ISBN 1-59296-176-2 (Lib. bdg. : alk. paper)
 1. Henry, Patrick, 1736–1799—Juvenile literature. 2. Legislators—United States—Biography—
Juvenile literature. 3. United States. Continental Congress—Biography—Juvenile literature.
4. Virginia—Politics and government—1775–1783—Juvenile literature. 5. United States—Politics
and government—1775–1783—Juvenile literature. [1. Henry, Patrick, 1736–1799. 2. Legislators.
3. United States—Politics and government—1775–1783.] I. Title. II. Series.
  E302.6.H5H45 2004
  973.3'092—dc22   2003018122

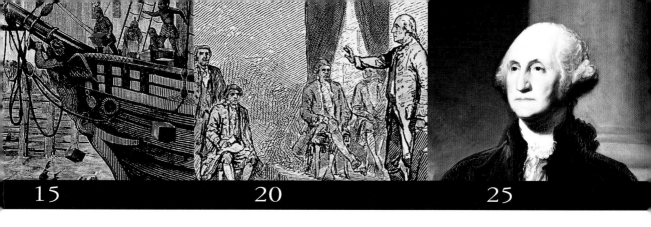

Contents

Chapter ONE

Seven Awesome Words

"GIVE ME LIBERTY OR GIVE ME DEATH!"

Patrick Henry is best known for speaking these seven words. He was ready to die for liberty. Others, he urged, must be ready as well.

Henry spoke these words in a fiery speech to Virginia colonists. He warned them that war was sure to

Patrick Henry delivers his famous "Give me liberty or give me death!" speech to colonists in Virginia.

break out at any moment. Great Britain had been forcing its American colonies to pay heavy taxes. Now the colonists were refusing to pay. They rioted and held other violent protests against unfair taxes. Redcoats—British soldiers—began roaming the streets in some colonies to keep order.

Henry knew that war was coming. The colonists, he said, must arm themselves and prepare. Surely death was better than losing their freedom. Sure enough, the Revolutionary War broke out in April 1775—just a month after Henry's speech.

Patrick Henry was known as the greatest orator, or public speaker, of his day. He proved that powerful

Interesting Fact

▶ Some colonists made images or dummies (called effigies) of British tax collectors and other officials. They hung the effigies in trees and often burned them to protest the taxes and frighten the officials.

words can change history. When people heard his speeches, they got moving! For Henry, the highest value was freedom. Freedom was a major theme in the Declaration of Independence, the Revolutionary War, and the Bill of Rights.

Henry was very different from other famous people of his time. He wasn't **polished,** like Thomas Jefferson. He wasn't stern and dignified, like George Washington. Nor was he a steady hard worker, like Benjamin Franklin. In fact, as a young man, Henry didn't seem very promising at all!

Patrick Henry was born on May 29, 1736, in Hanover County, Virginia. His parents were John and Sarah Winston Henry. Patrick was one of their nine children. He attended a local school until he was 10. Then his father taught him at home. He wouldn't study very hard, though. He preferred hunting, fishing, and roaming the fields. Even his friends said, "He loved idleness for its own sake."

When he was just 18 years old, he married Sarah Shelton. The first of their six chil-

Benjamin Franklin was a hard worker who excelled in the fields of printing, writing, science, and diplomacy.

dren was born a year later. Sarah's family had given the couple a tobacco plantation as a wedding gift. This seemed like a good start for the young couple, but it ended in disaster. The crops failed from **drought,** and a fire burned their house down.

Henry's father gave him money to open a store in 1757. Because of the drought, however, many people did not have money to be customers, and the business quickly failed. By now, Henry's relatives were getting fed up. They were afraid he was a good-for-nothing. His next job was working for his father-in-law in Hanover Tavern.

Right across the street from the tavern was the Hanover County Courthouse. In his spare time, Henry went to court and listened to the lawyers argue their cases. At last, he saw a place where he could make his mark in the world—and support his growing family. He began studying law in his spare time. In 1760, he traveled to Williamsburg, the capital of the Virginia Colony. There he passed his law exams, proudly earning a law license!

Henry took on a case called the Parsons' Cause in 1763. In this famous case, he criticized Britain's king for overturning a Virginia law. Henry brought up the idea of natural rights in his arguments. People are born with certain rights, he said, and no one can take them away. King George had taken away the colonists' rights, Henry declared. Such a king, he said, "degener-

In 1750, Virginia's population was about 230,000. About two out of five Virginians at that time were African-American slaves.

ates into a **tyrant,** and forfeits all right to his subjects' obedience."

Listeners in the courtroom were astonished at these daring words. When Henry won the case, the crowd broke out in cheers. They hoisted him up onto their shoulders and carried him to the tavern to celebrate. Henry's career as a brilliant public speaker had begun!

Patrick Henry argued that King George III (right) had taken away the colonists' rights and therefore had no right to expect their obedience.

In the 1700s, Virginia's economy depended on tobacco farming. Many Virginians owned huge tobacco plantations, and African-American slaves worked the fields. George Washington and Thomas Jefferson were among Virginia's plantation owners. People at their level of society were well educated and well dressed. They lived in fine mansions overlooking their lands.

Patrick Henry did not belong to Virginia's wealthy class. He understood the needs of the common people. That was one reason he took on the case of the Parsons' Cause.

In Virginia, tobacco was often used in place of money. The colony's farmers paid their Anglican ministers, or parsons, with tobacco. Because of ongoing drought, Virginia passed a law called the Two-Penny Act. It let the farmers pay the ministers in cash instead of tobacco if the crops were poor. This protected the farmers from losing what crops they had. The parsons protested to King George III, and the king threw out the law.

In court, Patrick Henry argued that the British king had no right to interfere with the colonists' laws. He won the case, and the amount of cash to be paid was set even lower than before. This victory made Henry a hero among Virginia's poor farmers.

A TOBACCO PLANTATION

Chapter TWO

Treason, Liberty, and Death

PATRICK HENRY WOULD SOON BE STIRRING UP
feelings throughout the colonies. In 1765, he was
elected to Virginia's House of Burgesses. That was

Patrick Henry was a member of the Virginia House of Burgesses, where he spoke out in favor of the colonists' right to make their own laws.

one house of the Virginia Assembly, which made the colony's laws. His election came just in time for an emergency.

That same year, Britain passed the Stamp Act. It forced new taxes on the colonists. They had to pay for tax stamps on newspapers, legal documents, college diplomas, and even playing cards.

At once, angry colonists discussed what to do about the Stamp Act. For Patrick Henry, the choice was clear. In a fiery speech before the House of Burgesses, he pushed the matter to the edge. The colonies had the right to make their own laws, he declared. They must cast off their unjust rule—just as others had done in the past. Henry went on to give examples.

"Caesar had his Brutus, Charles the First his Cromwell. . . ."

These were power-ful examples of famous overthrows. The ancient Roman emperor Julius Caesar had become a **dictator.** Brutus, one of Caesar's officers, murdered him.

The second example came closer to home. It was about King Charles I

Interesting Fact

▶ Thomas Jefferson was still a law student in 1765. However, he listened at the door as Patrick Henry gave his Caesar-Brutus speech. Jefferson said, "I . . . heard the splendid display of Mr. Henry's talents as a popular orator. They were great indeed; such as I have never heard from any other man."

Julius Caesar was killed by Brutus, one of his officers, on March 15, 44.

of England, who ruled in the 1600s. Oliver Crom-well led a **civil war** against King Charles. It led to the king's downfall and execution.

With these examples, Patrick Henry was just warming up. Now he was ready for the biggest shock of all.

"Caesar had his Brutus, Charles the First his Cromwell, and George the Third. . . ." At this point, Henry was interrupted by angry shouts. Many members of the House of Burgesses felt loyal to Britain's present king, George III.

"Treason! Treason!" they shouted. They were accusing Henry of trying to topple his government.

Nothing could stop Patrick Henry, though. He carried on. The king should learn from these examples, he said. An unjust leader is bound to be overthrown. "If this be treason, make the most of it!"

Henry proposed seven resolutions called the Virginia Stamp Act Resolutions. These said that only the colonists had the right to tax themselves. Copies of all of Henry's resolutions were printed in newspapers throughout the colonies. The House of Burgesses adopted four of the resolutions. Some say the Stamp Act Resolutions were the first steps toward the Revolutionary War.

Henry spent the next 10 years urging colonists to oppose the British. Meanwhile, one event after another brought them closer to war. In 1773,

colonists in Boston, Massachusetts, staged the Boston Tea Party. They dumped three shiploads of British tea overboard to protest the tea tax.

To punish Bostonians, Britain closed their port. Out of sympathy, Virginia's House of Burgesses declared a day of prayer and fasting. In response, Lord John Dunmore, Virginia's royal governor, closed down the Virginia Assembly.

The assembly members met anyway—in Williamsburg's Raleigh Tavern. They called for a meeting of all the colonies. That meeting took place in 1774 in Philadelphia, Pennsylvania. It was called the First Continental Congress. Henry attended, along with Virginians George Washington and Richard Henry Lee.

Virginia leaders met again in March 1775. This time, they gathered at St. John's Church in

The Sons of Liberty, a group of Patriots who were protesting the tax on tea, organized the Boston Tea Party.

Interesting Fact

▶ England was once a separate kingdom. The kingdoms of England, Scotland, and Wales were united in 1707. Together they formed the United Kingdom of Great Britain. Since 1922, the kingdom's full name has been the United Kingdom of Great Britain and Northern Ireland.

Lexington Green was the site of the battle that marked the beginning of the Revolutionary War.

Richmond. Everyone discussed what they should do next. For Patrick Henry, war was the only choice.

"If we wish to be free," he said, "we must fight! I repeat it, sir, we must fight! . . . The war is **inevitable**—and let it come!"

Finally, he brought his speech to a thundering close:

"Is life so dear, or peace so sweet, as to be purchased at the price of chains and slavery? Forbid it, Almighty God! I know not what course others may take, but as for me, give me liberty or give me death!"

According to reports at the time, no one applauded after this dazzling speech. Everyone just sat there for a moment, completely stunned. Henry's words had struck deeply into their minds and hearts.

Henry proposed resolutions for arming the Virginia **militia.** They would need guns and gunpowder in case of war with Britain. The convention passed his resolutions—and not a moment too soon. Just four weeks later—on April 19, 1775—Redcoats fired on militiamen in the Massachusetts towns of Lexington and Concord. Several colonists were killed. The Revolutionary War had begun.

PATRICK HENRY'S FAMOUS "LIBERTY OR DEATH" SPEECH IS MORE THAN 1,200 words long! The most famous lines come at the very end. However, many other parts of this speech are often quoted. Here is an example:

▸ "I have but one lamp by which my feet are guided, and that is the lamp of experience. I know of no way of judging of the future but by the past."

Here are famous lines from other Patrick Henry speeches:

▸ "I am not a Virginian, but an American."

▸ "Bad men cannot make good citizens."

▸ "I speak as one poor individual, but I speak the language of thousands."

▸ "The liberties of a people never were, nor ever will be, secure, when the transactions of their rulers may be concealed from them."

▸ "If we grant [the central government] too little power today, we can grant more tomorrow. But if we grant too much today, tomorrow will never come."

▸ "It is natural for man to indulge in the illusions of hope. We are apt to shut our eyes against a painful truth. . . . I am willing to know the whole truth, to know the worst, and to provide for it."

Chapter THREE

Fighting for Rights

WHEN THE REVOLUTION BROKE OUT, HENRY WAS MADE commander of the Virginia militia. He was soon back in **politics,** though. In 1776, he attended a convention that declared Virginia's independence

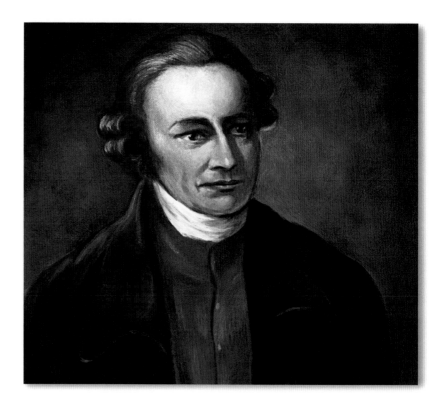

Patrick Henry was a well-respected leader in the Virginia colony who served as the commander of the Virginia militia and as the first governor of the colony after independence was declared.

and adopted a state constitution. This constitution included the Virginia Declaration of Rights. Henry had a part in writing it. Later that year, America's Declaration of Independence came out.

Members of the convention also elected Henry as the first governor of independent Virginia. He would serve three one-year terms in a row—the most allowed by Virginia law at the time. Henry made a big change in his personal life, too. His wife, Sarah, had died in 1775 after a long illness. In 1777, he married Dorothea Dandridge. They moved into the Governor's Palace in Williamsburg.

Henry was involved in Virginia's government for many more years. He returned to the legislature from 1780 to 1784. During this time, the Revolutionary War ended and a peace treaty was signed with Great Britain. He was governor again from 1784 to 1786. After his last term, the Henrys moved to a plantation called Leatherwood. It was in a county the citizens renamed Henry County after him. They promptly elected him to the Virginia legislature again.

As the new nation took shape, Henry had another big battle to fight. This time, his enemies were the Federalists. Federalists wanted a strong central government. Anti-Federalists were in favor of states' rights. Henry was one of the loudest voices among the Anti-Federalists.

Patrick Henry was not among the colonial leaders who attended the Constitutional Convention. He refused to attend the convention because he thought the Constitution would not be good for the young United States.

In 1787, each state chose representatives to the Constitutional Convention. They would meet in Philadelphia and draw up a Constitution. This document would describe how the government would be set up and how it would work.

Virginians chose Patrick Henry to attend the convention. He refused to go, however. According to some reports, he said, "I smell a rat" in Philadelphia. He didn't believe the Constitution would be good for the nation.

Once the Constitution was written, it was sent to the states for approval. Conventions met in each state to debate the Constitution and take a vote. At

ALEXANDER HAMILTON, JAMES MADISON, AND JOHN JAY WERE LEADING
Federalists in the 1780s. They wrote 85 articles in favor of the Constitution.
These articles were collected and published together as *The Federalist Papers.*
Their purpose was to convince people that the U.S. Constitution was good for
the country.

In response, Anti-Federalists published another flurry of articles. These are
called the *Anti-Federalist Papers.* Some of the authors were Edmund Randolph
and George Mason of Virginia. The Anti-Federalists had many complaints and
fears. Some of them are listed below.

▸ The Constitution gives too much power to the central government.
▸ The president would be like a king.
▸ The wealthy upper classes would have the most power.
▸ America is too vast to be ruled by a central government.
▸ The government would control business and trade.
▸ People would not have control over their own local affairs.
▸ The government's power to send troops would keep people from struggling for freedom.

Anti-Federalists believed that Americans needed
protection from these dangers. They needed a
guarantee of individual rights. This led to the
Bill of Rights.

What do you think? Discuss the Anti-
Federalists' concerns and compare them to life
in the United States today.

THE

FEDERALIST:

ADDRESSED TO THE

PEOPLE OF THE STATE OF
NEW-YORK.

NUMBER I.

Introduction.

AFTER an unequivocal experience of the ineffi-
cacy of the subsisting federal government, you
are called upon to deliberate on a new constitution for
the United States of America. The subject speaks its
own importance; comprehending in its consequences,
nothing less than the existence of the UNION, the
safety and welfare of the parts of which it is com-
posed, the fate of an empire, in many respects, the
most interesting in the world. It has been frequently
remarked, that it seems to have been reserved to the
people of this country, by their conduct and example,
to decide the important question, whether societies of
men are really capable or not, of establishing good
government from reflection and choice, or whether
they are forever destined to depend, for their political
constitutions, on accident and force. If there be any
truth in the remark, the crisis, at which we are arrived,
may with propriety be regarded as the æra in which
A   that

Alexander Hamilton, leader of the Federalists, believed the country needed a strong central government and argued in favor of the new Constitution.

once, Federalists and Anti-Federalists were in heated debate. Federalists believed the Constitution assured liberty and justice for all. Anti-Federalists saw the Constitution in quite a different way. They believed it threatened the freedom Americans had just won from Britain.

Patrick Henry was concerned about the poor farmers of Virginia. He believed their rights would be overlooked if the central government were too powerful. At the Virginia Convention of 1788, he spoke out strongly against the Constitution. He said it "has an awful squinting—it squints toward **monarchy.**" He believed it would make the United States a kingdom, just like Great Britain. "Your president may easily become king; your senate . . . may be a small minority." And the result would be horrible: "If a wrong step be now made, the republic will be lost forever!"

Henry insisted that the Constitution include a Bill of Rights. This would protect individual liberties. Many citizens of Virginia and other states agreed. Only when this was promised did Virginia vote "yes" on the Constitution. The Bill of Rights was approved in 1791. It consisted of the first 10 **amendments,** or changes, to the U.S. Constitution.

Interesting Fact

▶ Today, the Constitution has 27 amendments.

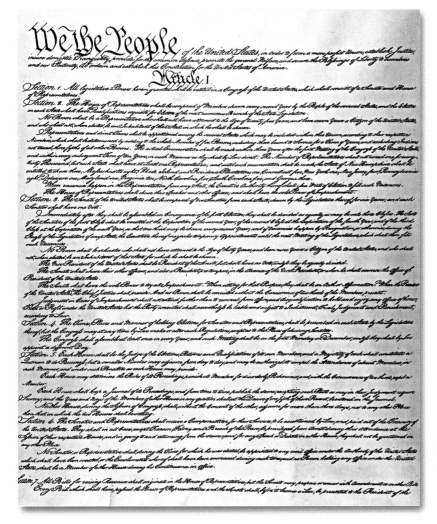

Virginia finally agreed to vote for the U.S. Constitution after it was agreed that a Bill of Rights that protected individual liberties would be added to the document.

Chapter FOUR

United We Stand

Red Hill was the home of Patrick Henry from 1794 until his death in 1799.

IN 1794, PATRICK HENRY MOVED HIS FAMILY TO Red Hill, an estate in Charlotte County, Virginia. He wanted to stay home, practice law, and enjoy his family. With Dorothea, Henry had a "second family" of 11 children!

Henry was still in great demand, though. He had many offers to get back into politics. George

Washington, the nation's first president, admired Henry. The two were also old friends. Washington asked him to be secretary of state in 1795 and chief justice of the U.S. Supreme Court in 1796. However, Henry refused them both. He also refused an offer to run for governor again.

John Adams, the second president, asked Henry to be U.S. minister to France in 1799.

Interesting Fact

▸ Today's Republican Party began in 1854 in Ripon, Wisconsin. It was made up of people opposed to slavery and people who wanted to settle western lands.

By now, however, Henry was in poor health. He refused this post, too.

Henry still kept his eye on politics. He especially watched Thomas Jefferson, his fellow Virginian. Jefferson opposed the Federalists as much as Henry did. He disagreed with many views of George Washington and John Adams—both Federalists. Jefferson formed his own political party, called the Democratic-Republican Party. It led to today's Democratic Party.

In 1799, George Washington persuaded Henry to run for the Virginia legislature again. This time, he was eager to do it. The Alien and Sedition Acts had just been passed. They made it a crime to criticize the government. Newspaper writers and politicians were in grave danger if they spoke their minds.

Thomas Jefferson and the Democratic-Republicans were outraged. They said these acts gave the federal government too much power. Jefferson and James Madison drew up the Virginia and Kentucky Resolutions. These measures would give the states tremendous power. States would be able to decide whether a national law was in line with the Constitution or not. If not, the states would be free to disobey the law.

Patrick Henry hated the Alien and Sedition Acts. He also opposed the Virginia and Kentucky Resolutions, however. If they passed, the states

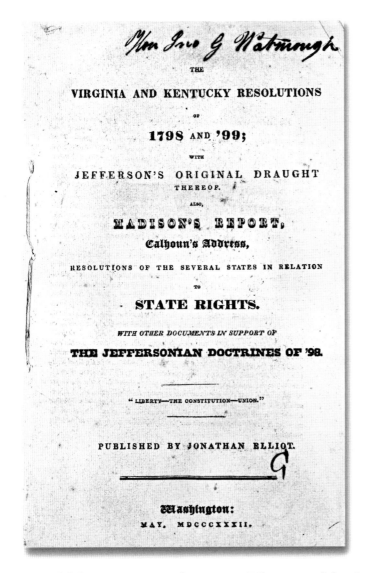

THE

VIRGINIA AND KENTUCKY RESOLUTIONS

OF

1798 AND '99;

WITH

JEFFERSON'S ORIGINAL DRAUGHT
THEREOF.

ALSO,

MADISON'S REPORT,

Calhoun's Address,

RESOLUTIONS OF THE SEVERAL STATES IN RELATION

TO

STATE RIGHTS.

WITH OTHER DOCUMENTS IN SUPPORT OF

THE JEFFERSONIAN DOCTRINES OF '98.

"LIBERTY—THE CONSTITUTION—UNION."

PUBLISHED BY JONATHAN ELLIOT.

Washington:
MAY, MDCCCXXXII.

The Virginia and Kentucky Resolutions would give each state the power to decide whether or not national laws were to be observed by the people of the state. These resolutions were never passed.

would have *too much* power. They could wipe out the authority of the U.S. government. For Henry, this was going too far. He had to return to the legislature and get involved.

In March 1799, Henry gave a campaign speech on the steps of Charlotte Courthouse. He called for Americans to stick together. "United we stand, divided we fall," he said. "Let us not split into factions that would destroy the Union upon which our existence hangs."

Sadly, this was the last public speech Henry would ever make. He won the election, but he would never take his seat in the legislature. He died on June 6, 1799, and was buried on his Red Hill estate.

Patrick Henry would have been pleased to know that the Alien and Sedition Acts were repealed, and the Virginia and Kentucky Resolutions never became law. Americans had made the right decision after all: "United we stand."

Patrick Henry is remembered as a great orator and respected leader who helped create the United States of America.

1736   Patrick Henry is born on May 29 in Hanover County, Virginia.

1760   Henry begins practicing law.

1765   Henry is elected to the Virginia House of Burgesses; he proposes resolutions defying the Stamp Act.

1774   Henry attends the First Continental Congress in Philadelphia, Pennsylvania.

1775   On March 23, Henry gives his famous "Liberty or Death" speech at St. John's Church in Richmond, Virginia; he serves as a Virginia militia leader.

1776–1779   Henry serves as the first governor of independent Virginia.

1784–1786   Henry is governor of Virginia again.

1787   Henry refuses to attend the Constitutional Convention; as an Anti-Federalist, he strongly opposes the Constitution.

1788   Henry is elected to the Virginia House of Delegates and the Virginia Convention of 1788; his arguments lead to the Constitution's Bill of Rights.

1791   The Bill of Rights is approved.

1794   Henry moves to his Red Hill estate near Brookneal, Virginia.

1799   Henry dies at Red Hill on June 6 at the age of 63.

Glossary TERMS

amendments (uh-MEND-muhnts)
Amendments are changes or additions to something. Patrick Henry wanted a Bill of Rights added to the Constitution, and it became the Constitution's first 10 amendments.

civil war (SIV-il WOR)
A civil war is a war fought between opposing forces within a country. In his "Caesar-Brutus" speech, Henry mentioned Oliver Cromwell, who led a civil war against King Charles I.

dictator (DIK-tay-tur)
A dictator is a ruler who takes total power and often rules a country unfairly. In his "Caesar-Brutus" speech, Henry compared the Roman dictator Caesar to King George III.

drought (DROUT)
A drought is a long spell of very dry weather. Patrick Henry's crops failed because of a drought.

inevitable (in-EV-uh-tuh-buhl)
An event that cannot be prevented is inevitable. In his "Liberty or Death" speech, Henry declared that war was inevitable.

militia (muh-LISH-uh)
A militia is a group of citizens armed for protection. Henry urged Virginia's legislature to provide arms for its militia to fight the British.

monarchy (MON-ar-kee)
A monarchy is the rule of a king. Henry refused to attend the 1787 Constitutional Convention because he believed the Constitution would make the United States a monarchy.

polished (POL-isht)
Someone who is polished is confident and well-spoken. As a young man, Patrick Henry was not polished.

politics (POL-uh-tiks)
Politics is the study or practice of government. Henry was involved in politics for most of his life.

tyrant (TY-ruhnt)
A tyrant is a harsh and cruel ruler. In arguing the Parsons' Cause, Henry said a ruler who takes away the people's rights is a tyrant.

For Further INFORMATION

Web Sites

Visit our home page for lots of links about Patrick Henry:
http://www.childsworld.com/links.html

Note to Parents, Teachers, and Librarians:
We routinely verify our Web links to make sure they're safe,
active sites—so encourage your readers to check them out!

Books

Grote, JoAnn A., *Patrick Henry.* Philadelphia: Chelsea House Publishers, 1999.

Kukla, Amy, and Jon Kukla. *Patrick Henry: Voice of the Revolution.* New York: PowerKids Press Books, 2002.

McPherson, Stephanie Sammartino, and Nicolas Debon (illustrator). *Liberty or Death: A Story about Patrick Henry.* Minneapolis: Carolrhoda Books, 2002.

Places to Visit or Contact

Red Hill, the Patrick Henry National Memorial
To tour Patrick Henry's last home and burial place
1250 Red Hill Road
Brookneal, VA 24528
800/514-7463
www.redhill.org

St. John's Episcopal Church
To see where Patrick Henry gave his famous "Liberty or Death" speech
2401 East Broad Street
Richmond, VA 23223
804/648-5015

Index

About the Author

ANN HEINRICHS GREW UP IN FORT SMITH, ARKANSAS, AND LIVES in Chicago. She is the author of more than 100 books for children and young adults on U.S. and world history. After many years as a children's book editor, she enjoyed a successful career as an advertising copywriter. Ms. Heinrichs has traveled extensively throughout the United States, Africa, Asia, and the Middle East. She is also an award-winning martial artist.